Object Lessons
for
Christian Growth

Wesley T. Runk

D1519408

BAKER BOOK HOUSE
Grand Rapids, Michigan

Formerly published under the title,
Growing Up in God

© 1973 by C.S.S. Publishing Co.,
Lima, Ohio

Reprinted 1974 by
Baker Book House Company
ISBN: 0-8010-7629-3

First printing, January 1975
Second printing, October 1977

PHOTOLITHOPRINTED BY CUSHING - MALLOY, INC.
ANN ARBOR, MICHIGAN, UNITED STATES OF AMERICA
1977

CONTENTS

A SPECIAL GIFT

Titus 3:4-7, verse 7: "He did this so that we should be justified by his grace, to become heirs looking forward to inheriting eternal life."

Object: A piece of fine china, a beautiful book, and a piece of fine jewelry.

Good morning, boys and girls. How are you on such a lovely day as this first Sunday of the new year? Just think, the world is another year older by our count. There are different ideas about getting old, depending upon whom you talk to. How many of the boys and girls here this morning would like to be 16 years old? A lot of you? How many wish you were only two years old? Not very many want to be two years old. You want to grow up to be older than you are now.

Older people like your moms and dads joke a lot about getting older. Someday when we get so old, we will leave this world and go to live with God in a very special way. I want to talk to you about that special way in a little while. But first I want to tell you something else. When we go to God we have to do something with all the things we have collected during our time here on earth. For instance, I wouldn't want to just break up these beautiful dishes that I have here.They are hand-painted and beautifully made. The same is true about this very interesting book with a leather cover that is part of a big library. I don't want to burn all of the books. And what should I do with this gorgeous jewel, just throw it away? Of course not! I would give these things, if they were mine, to my children. The grown-up word is "heirs."

The person who has these beautiful things can choose to

give them to whomever he wants. Most of the time parents give their possessions to their children before they go to live with God.

Now I told you that when people go to God at the time of death, God makes special arrangements. You remember that things were not always so good between God and man. When man sins he turns away from God. But when Jesus came he cleared things up pretty well. So well, in fact, that before Jesus went to the cross and died he wanted to leave something with all of his friends. It was something that only he could give. Jesus didn't have money or jewels or books or dishes, but he had something that no one else could give. That gift was called **life,** eternal life. That is why we have special arrangements with God, because Jesus chose to give us eternal life as his special gift. Now you know why older people don't mind dying, because they know God has a brand new life waiting for them, made possible by very special arrangements. That means we are the heirs of Jesus because he gave us what he had to give before he died: life, eternal life.

CHANGING STYLES

Romans 12:1-5, verse 2: "Don't copy the fashions and customs of this world, but be a new and different person with a fresh newness in all you do and think. Then you will see from your own experience how His ways will really satisfy you."

Object: Different styles representing different periods such as ties, shoes and hats. The aim is to show how the ways of the world change but not God's expression of love.

Good morning to you, models. This morning we have a brand new experience for you in worship. How many of you have ever been clothes models before? None of you!! Well, today some of you are going to be models. I need some very strong and handsome boys and some beautiful young ladies. [Select some volunteers. A good time to take some of the children who would not be selected by the aforementioned description in schools.] Oh, that's fine. First of all, we are going to use the boys because we are going to model neckties. [Select a bow tie, a wide tie, a very thin one and maybe even a short string tie. Have them look fairly ridiculous by arranging them too long or short.] My, oh, my, you boys do look good. Now let's try the girls with some beautiful hats. [Repeat the experiment using bonnets and wide brims, pillbox hats, with and without veils, etc.[What beautiful ladies! Perhaps the boys and girls would each like to select a pair of shoes that would go well with their hats and neckties. [Boots, galoshes, patent leather, high heels, paratrooper boots, etc.[

That's lovely. My, how times change! Would you believe, boys and girls, that a long time ago people would not go outside unless they had a bonnet like this or a wide tie like that or a pair of beautiful looking shoes like this? Everyone had to wear the same kind of thing or it was just terrible. We are still like that about our styles. We still think that we must wear the same kind of clothes that everyone else wears.

We are also like that about our sinning. Very often when one boy does something bad another boy thinks he should do the same thing. One little girl tells a lie and her friend tells her mother the same lie. One boy says a bad word and lots of boys say the same bad word.

St. Paul says, "Don't do it!" Don't try to be like everyone else and their sinning. Instead he says, "Turn to God and see what He can do for you." God has different ways of showing you His love and when He loves you so that you know it, then you will want to be like Him and not like the one who is trying to make you sin. God's ways don't change like the styles of ties, shoes and hats. God's way is love and there is so much of it that everyone can have as much as he wants and there will still be a lot left over.

USING OUR SPECIAL TALENTS

Romans 12:6-16a, verse 6a: "God has given each of us the ability to do certain things well."

Object: Cup, scissors, picture.

Good morning, boys and girls. How are you on this beautiful winter morning? Winter must be a very special season for God, because He decorates His earth with snow and beautiful cloud formations in the heavens. It is wonderful how the various seasons do different things and make us feel differently. It makes me think of some good friends around my house that have special jobs. Let me show you what I mean.

First of all there is my friend, Charley Cup. [**Hold up cup, admiring it as a friend.**] Good old Charley lets me drink my milk out of him every morning and once in a while, if I ask politely, he even lets me dunk a donut or a roll in him. Good old Charley.

Have you ever met Sally Scissors? [**Hold up scissors.**] Sally is quite anxious to please me, and she helps me cut up paper and string. I never have to worry about the neatness of a project when Sally is on the job.

I want you to meet one other friend. His name is Pat Picture, and what a quiet friend he is! Pat never says much, but just hangs on the wall and gives all of my friends a good time by just being there where they can look at him.

All of my friends have special talents. Do you know what the word **talent** means? [**Let them answer.**] A talent is something that a person can do well. Charles can hold milk, and Sally can cut paper, and Pat is handsome to look at. Not everyone has the same talent. Can you imagine how good Sally would be at holding my milk? Do you think Pat would do very well at cutting paper? How would you like to have Charley hanging on the wall? It wouldn't work out very well, would it?

That's the way it is in Christ's Church. God makes all of us different so that we can all help Him teach other children. To some He gives the talent to make people feel good, and to others He has given strength so that they can protect us. One talent is just as important as the other, because God made it. But we must use our talents and use them well. Do you remember how good Charley was at hanging on the wall? Not very good, was he? But when he is filled with milk he is terrific.

You can be like Charley and Sally and Pat and work hard at using the talents that God has given you. If you use your special talents well, you will not only please God, but your friends and family as well.

CHRISTIAN CHAMPIONS

I Corinthians 9:24-10:5, verse 27: I treat my body hard and make it obey me, for, having been an announcer myself, I should not want to be disqualified.

Object: Exercises; calisthenics.

Good morning, champions, and how are you today? Some of you look a little soft in the muscles and around your tummies. Boy, it is hard to be a champion if you are not in A-1 shape. That's right. We need strong bodies to be champions, and to have strong bodies we must really work hard. Let me show you what I mean. [**If you have a member of your congregation, a high school boy or young man, who would do this it would really help; if not, do very simple exercises that can be started by the pastor.**] Everybody stand up. Keep your knees straight and bend over and touch your toes. Oh, my, this group of champions is really out of shape. Raise your hands high over your head and then bend at your waist and touch your toes. That's better. Let's try some more and you follow my count: 1,2,3,4 ... Again and again. Now, fast, faster, faster. Oh, my, some of you are really out of shape!

You know, that is the way some people who think they are Christians act. They talk about being Christians but they are so badly out of shape that they almost slip right out of God's Kingdom.

Jesus teaches us to pray so that we can talk to God often. These Christians forget to pray and then when they need to they don't know how. God gave us the Holy Bible so that the really important things that we need to know about would be kept in one place that we can find it

9

easily and then these people forget to read it. And God gave us a place to come together and worship and make good Christian friends, and then we forget to come to church.

Pretty soon we are as out of shape as Christians as we are as champions. You know how it hurts to stretch our muscles. Some people find it just as hard to get out of bed on Sunday morning or wait to thank God before they eat.

So we want to be like St. Paul tells us to be. We want to thank God and get back in shape as Christians so that we don't slip right out of God's Kingdom. Let's not forget to do the things that God tells us will help us remain strong in our faith and love of God.

GOD MAKES US STRONG

2 Corinthians 11:19-12:9, verse 9: But he said to me, "My grace is sufficient for you, for my power is made perfect in weakness." I will all the more gladly boast of my weaknesses, that the power of Christ may rest upon me.

Object: A sack of something like cement or other material that would be too heavy for a child to lift, but could be lifted by the pastor.

Well, here we are safely through the month of January and at church on the very first Sunday of February. February is really a fun month because of all the special days in it, and also because it is the shortest month in the year.

I have brought with me this morning what I hope will also be a very fun kind of children's sermon which will also help us to learn something about Jesus and the way he wants us to think of him.

Do you see this big sack that I have brought with me this morning? You have probably seen bigger sacks, but I want to tell you that it is one of the heaviest sacks I have ever carried. Now, someone told me before I came in that there were probably some of the strongest boys and girls here that there are anywhere, so I thought that I would test them out to see just how strong you really are. I need some volunteers to do this particular experiment. **[Choose some volunteers.]**

Well, here they are, the young people I have heard so much about, whom everyone says are so strong. **[Let them try to lift it up off the ground, but warn them not to strain or hurt themselves. If they do get it up simply ask**

them to hold it there for a few minutes.] My, this is a heavy sack, isn't it? It would be hard for any one of us to carry it for a long distance, wouldn't it? Now, if one of our volunteers would please stay here we are going to try something else. You are going to lift it this time but I am going to help you and we will see if it goes any easier. Are you ready? Lift. Wonderful! Terrific! Now you can see how much easier it is when we get the kind of help that we need. You become strong when I help you and we get the job done.

That's the way it is for the Christian when he asks and gets help from Christ. We are all weak when it comes to being good people, worthy of belonging to God's Kingdom. Even the smallest job that God gives us is too big if we do not let Him help us. St. Paul had another way of saying it when he said, "Christ's power is made perfect in our weakness." We really know what strength we have when someone helps us do a job that we are not able to do by ourselves.

So, just as when I helped you lift the heavy sack, you used my strength to help you lift it, so Christ makes us good not by what we do but by doing it for us. And one other thing that is important is this: it is nothing to ashamed of to let Jesus help us with our spiritual problems. God wants us to pray to Him for our help and when we get it we will be glad and strong.

A BETTER WAY

I Corinthians 13:1-13, verse 10: But when the perfect comes, the imperfect will pass away.

Object: Two methods of doing the same thing, one much more efficiently than the other.

Good morning, boys and girls. Look what I brought with me to show you. What is it? That's right, a camera. Good old Candy Camera, one of my oldest and dearest friends. Candy has been taking pictures for me for a lot of years. Let me show you how. First of all, I get you all lined up and then I move a little bit this way and a little bit that way and then I check and make sure that I have enough light and then I look back and see if I can still see you and turn this so that I have you right in focus and then I snap old Candy Camera and pray that it took a good picture. Of course, I can't be too sure because I have to turn the roll to just the right place and then take it to the store and have it developed and then if everything is just right I will be able to see you in a print.

On the other hand, I brought another one of my friends, Ichabod Instamatic. With my good friend Ichabod I just look through one little window and snap the picture. Everything else is done by the camera. Of course, I still have to take it to the store. But there is another friend whom I am sure you all know called Polly Polaroid who not only takes your picture but also shows it to you within ten seconds.

Well, now, what does all this mean? Let me show you. There are a lot of good people in this world. They obey the laws and do nice things for other people and are pretty happy. But some of them are missing one thing.

They don't know Christ and the love of Christ, so they don't have it all. They are like the first friend, Candy, who does a lot of things, but for some reason seems to be missing something. This is the way that everyone had to be before Jesus came. They could try very hard and have a lot but they were missing something and that something was the love of Christ. Christ's love is for boys and girls and it does so much more yet requires no effort on our part. It comes from heaven and is given to us freely. We don't even have to wait to see if it works. It always works and it is always good.

You may know a lot of good people, but they are not what they could be unless they have the love of Christ. And that love is the very best thing in the world at any time.

ROADBLOCKS TO JESUS

2 Corinthians 6:1-10, verse 3: We put no obstacle in anyone's way, so that no fault may be found with our ministry.

Object: A saw horse with a big detour sign printed and hung on it.

Today is a good day to be together for it is God's day. When I was thinking about our children's sermon for this Sunday, I could not help but think of this verse in our lesson for today: "We put no obstacle in anyone's way, so that no fault may be found with our ministry." I thought and thought of how I could show you what that verse meant, and I finally thought of a way.

Do you see that aisle that runs right down the middle of the church and leads up to the altar? Let's suppose for a minute that the aisle is the street and the only way that you can get to Jesus. Now if you want to know God any better, you must follow that street. But suppose we take this old sawhorse and put it right here in front of the steps leading to the altar and hang a sign on it that says, **DETOUR -- GO ANOTHER WAY.** That means that anybody walking down this street cannot make it to the altar to know Jesus. We have blocked it off just as the highway workmen do when they are working on the road ahead. That means nobody can get through.

Sometimes though, it is not a sawhorse with a sign on it that keeps people from getting to God's altar and knowing Jesus better. Sometimes it is a different kind of obstacle or roadblock. Let me show you what I mean. **[Take away the sawhorse and keep the sign, then select one of the children to come up and stand in the same**

place that the sawhorse stood.] Now we are going to pretend that Jimmy is the kind of a Christian who doesn't obey his parents and never forgives his friends and hates to help anyone who asks him and always wishes that he had what somebody else was given instead of what was given to him. When Jimmy is like that we might as well hang the **DETOUR —— GO ANOTHER WAY** sign on him. This Jimmy tells people that he is a Christian and loves God, but look at the way he acts and thinks. When people see him, they don't want to have anything to do with his Jesus or God.

Do you understand what I mean? We can keep people from wanting to be Christians if we don't remember that wherever we go and whatever we do we are watched by others to see if we really believe in our God and love others as He teaches us to love.

Too many boys and girls and moms and dads are like the roadblock sign that keeps people from coming to know Jesus. They block the road just as the sign and sawhorse did the center aisle in the church. They keep people from knowing Jesus where they go to school, or at play or at work. That's what St. Paul meant when he said, "We put no obstacle in anyone's way, so that no fault may be found with our ministry."

I hope that you can remember this and not be a sawhorse with a detour sign. But instead we want you to be wide open roads that lead people to Jesus and a better understanding of God.

GROWING UP IN GOD

1 Thessalonians 4:1-7, verse 1: Finally, brethren, we beseech and exhort you in the Lord Jesus, that as you learned from us how you ought to live and to please God, just as you are doing, you do so more and more.

Object: Any series of books that increase in difficulty, e.g., 1st grade arithmetic, 4th grade arithmetic, algebra, trigonometry, etc.

Today is really a special day. First, it is God's day and that makes it special. Secondly, we are close to the birthday of our first president of the United States, George Washington. He is remembered as a man who was very honest. I think that he would like to be remembered that way better than any other way. Did you know St. Paul was always concerned about how people lived and that what they learned from God they put into practice right away? We are always learning and when we learn to do something better we do it the new way rather than the old.

Look what I have here. These are some arithmetic books that I collected at the school to show you how you learn. Here is the first grade book. For first graders it is really hard. It takes a long time to remember all the numbers. Here is the 4th grade book. See how things have changed. The printed words are smaller and so are the numbers, because they have to get so much more in the books. Now the boys and girls are learning to add and subtract and divide and work word problems and all sorts of things. Look at this book if you want to see a hard one. This came from the high school and it is called algebra. Boy, look at how hard this is! I don't think that a fifth grader could do this work. Finally I brought a college book called calculus. If you think the other was hard, let me tell you that this looks like a foreign language. Well, what is this all about and what does it have to do with God's day?

St. Paul taught us that we are not only supposed to grow up in our size and our mind but that we are also supposed to grow up in the way we live, always taking on more and more responsibilities. When we are very little we fight with our brothers and sisters but then when we get a little older and hear what Jesus teaches us about fighting we quit and try to solve our problems another way by talking them out. When we are little we have moms and dads who do all the work around the house but when we grow up a little bit we decide that we should help and do the kind of jobs that we can do well. Then there is the boy or girl who is a little different than we are and we are not so sure when we are little if we ought to play with him because he is different. Maybe he is not as smart, or of the same color or seems to be very poor or have something wrong with his body. We feel differently towards him than we do our other friends. But when we grow up and listen to what Jesus teaches us we know that those are exactly the kinds of people that Jesus wanted us to help and make friends with.

Now, I don't know how grown up all of you are as Christians. You see, an age like six or seven doesn't really matter here because you can be fifty years old and still be a baby Christian or you could be five years old and be a pretty grown up Christian. The thing that is important is that when you learn how a Christian lives his life and learns to love and help everybody, then you must not just know it but also do it. That is how a Christian grows up in God and is always glad that he has learned from God how to live.

18

EMPTY WORDS — — EMPTY CUPS

Ephesians 5:1-9, verse 6: Let no one deceive you with empty words, for it is because of these things that the wrath of God comes upon the sons of disobedience.

Object: Some paper cups filled with water and one empty cup.

Good morning, boys and girls. Do you know what special day is coming soon? EASTER, that's right. We certainly want to be ready for that day, don't we? We have to study and pray and listen to what is said about Jesus and the great day of Easter. Most of all, we have to take what we read and hear and say and make certain that it helps to change our hearts toward Jesus.

Let me show you what I mean about words and how they can affect us. How many of you get a little thirsty sometimes when you sit in church this long? Oh, my, a lot of you. That's what I thought. I just happened to bring along with me this morning a nice big pitcher of water and some paper cups so that while I am talking to you about Jesus you might enjoy a cup of water. Let me pour, and I will just hand them out to you and while I am doing that you listen to me carefully. [**Begin to pass out the cups of water to some of the children and talk about how important it is to do what we say we are going to do. Every now and then give one or two of the children an empty cup. Hopefully you will choose a child who will not call your attention immediately to the fact that he did not get any water in his cup.**] Now boys and girls, it is very important that we do what we say we are going to do. If we promise to bring in the paper at night then we should bring in the paper, or if we say that we are going to practice our piano lesson for so long, we should do it that long. If we promise a friend that we will be over to help him paint the fence, then we should not let him down. Whatever we say that we will do we should do, because people depend on our doing what we say we are going to do.

God is like that also, for He wants to be able to count on our doing what we say we will do. When we promise to be servants of Christ and live as Christ wants us to live, then God expects Christians will be followers of Christ and do what a Christian says he will do. You understand what I mean, don't you? If I promised you that I would give you a cup of water, you expect to have water in your cup, don't you? You wouldn't like it if some of you were promised water in your cup and then I didn't give it to you. Did anybody get an empty cup? Oh, my heavens! Did you really get an empty cup? Do you feel that I betrayed you, or let you down or did you enjoy drinking from an empty cup?

Now you understand what it is like to say something and not mean it. Words can be just as empty as cups, can't they, if the words are not backed up by our actions. Anyone can promise you anything. I could promise you a million dollars but if I don't have a million dollars then my words are empty. I can promise you a cup of water but if I don't give you water in your cup my words are empty.

So let me fill your cups and you promise God and all of your friends that you will only tell them something when you intend to do it. Then God and other people will count on you. No more empty words, but words filled with action to back up what you say.

CHILDREN OF PROMISE

Galatians 4:21-5:1a, verse 28: Now we, brethren, like Isaac, are children of promise.

Object: Boy scout pin, girl scout pin.

Good morning to you, boys and girls. How are you on this God's day? I love Sunday morning when you wake up and know that in a few hours you will be standing in a special place made for worship and singing songs of praise to God who loves you and cares for you all of the day. It makes you feel good, like when you tell your mother or father, "I love you, Mom," or "I love you, Dad," and they get a big smile on their faces and bend down and give you a kiss. Doesn't that make you feel great?

We have a special story, but I wanted to tell you how much I enjoy being with you on this Sunday and every Sunday. Look what I brought with me today. These are very special pins and they mean something very special to every boy and girl who has one. Do you know who wears pins like these? That's right, this is a boy scout pin and this one is a girl scout pin. Does everyone have one of these pins? No, not everyone. You have to be a boy scout or a girl scout to have one of these pins, and not every boy or every girl is a scout. But you know what this pin means to the boy or the girl who is a scout. Does it mean that they are very strong? Does it mean that they are very smart? Does it mean that they have brown hair? No, it doesn't mean any of those things. Let me tell you what it means. It means that they have made a promise to keep a certain law, called the scout law. They promise to do their best and help a lot of other people. They are special people because they have a special promise to keep.

Did you know that Christians are a special people also because of a promise? That's right, we are, as Christians, called the children of promise. It started a long time ago, long before there were any boy scouts or girl scouts. Thousands of years ago God said that we would be a special people, a people to whom He would make a special promise. Now the reason I am telling you this is that sometimes you may think that it is hard to tell the difference between people who are Christians and people who are not Christians. Boys and girls and mothers and fathers who are not Christians eat food, wear clothes and ride in cars and live in houses and talk and sing and laugh and cry just as you and I do.

It is very hard to tell the difference. Christians do not wear pins like scouts or special clothes so that you can tell them apart from others, but I want to tell you something that Christians do have that no one else has: a promise from God. That's right, you and I have a promise that is made at the time that we are baptized and made part of God's family. That promise is that God will care for us. You can't always tell who the children of promise are except that God says that people who love God also love people and many times you know Christians just by the way that they love others.

Oh, there is one other thing that maybe you have seen that is kind of like a sign for Christians. Do you know what it might be? It is a special sign that is in every Christian church and it is something that Jesus once had to carry on his back. A cross, that's right. That is the sign of Christianity, just as this boy scout pin is the sign of Boy Scouting and this one is for Girl Scouting. That cross is a promise from God to man that said, "I forgive your sins and I welcome you back into my family. You are my children of promise."

GOD'S PLAN TO BRING US TOGETHER

Hebrews 9:11-15, verse 15: Therefore he is the mediator of a new covenant, so that those who are called may receive the promised eternal inheritance, since a death has occurred which redeems them from the transgressions under the first covenant.

Object: Two pieces of cloth, one with a button, one with a buttonhole.

Good morning, boys and girls. It is good to see you on this Sunday. I know that you know that it is important to worship God and to tell Him how much you love Him. I want you to know that not only does God miss you when you are not here, but so do I. You are really important to me and to our church, as well as to God.

A long time ago it was very difficult for God and His children, the people of this world, to get together. Something had happened a long time ago that separated God from His people. Oh, it wasn't that God didn't care. He did. He really did care a lot. As a matter of fact, God tried hundreds of times to bring His people back to Him and make them loving and obedient children again, but they just never seemed to want to stay with Him very long. I guess many of the people didn't really understand or believe that God cared as much as He did. You remember Moses and the Ten Commandments and Noah and the rainbow. Well, all those were ways that God tried through some special people to let His children know that He really did care and love them. It would work for a little while and then the first thing you know the people would forget all about it and go off and either worship some fake God or just forget altogether. God knew that some day He would have to have something very special so that He and His people could come back together again.

Let me show you what I mean. You see these two pieces of cloth that I have with me? They look very much alike, you might even say that one was a copy of the other or both of them were made from the same pattern. Well, these two pieces of cloth want very much to be together, but they can only be kept together as long as I am holding them here. If I take my hands off, one piece just falls away. What we need is something that will connect them so that they will never fall apart again. Let's pretend that one of these pieces is God and the other piece, made in the same image, is a child of God like you or me.

Now the first piece says, "I know what we need so that we can come together again. I will send a button to the other piece of cloth," and so he does. [**Here is the place for someone to sew a button to the piece without the buttonhole, if not already done.**] Then He says, "I am going to give that button a name." Now the first piece of cloth called the button Benny. So Benny brought the two pieces of cloth together and they could not come apart again.

Well, boys and girls, I know what you are thinking and you are right. Jesus is like Benny the button and God is like the first piece of cloth that sent Benny. God sent Jesus to bring Himself and His children back together again. Jesus is like a button. He is the mediator or the Bringer- together. What a wonderful planner God is and His gift of Jesus is magnificent. We are so grateful for what He has done. Now you can remember every time you see a button that God had a wonderful plan to bring us back together again through Jesus.

V.I.P.'S

**Philippians 2:5-11, verse 9: Therefore God has highly
exalted Him and bestowed on Him the name which is
above every name.**

**Object: A series of cards that can be taped to a board.
The names should be Richard Nixon, Joe Namath, Fred
Flintstone, Neil Armstrong, The Beatles, the pastor's
name, one of the children's names.**
Card with the word JESUS held till appropriate time.

Good morning, boys and girls. How are you on this
wonderful Sunday called Palm Sunday? It is only a week
away from what Sunday? That's right, Easter Sunday,
the most special Sunday of all. But Palm Sunday is a very
special day, too. It begins something that we call Holy
Week, a time when we remember the last days of Jesus'
life with both great sorrow and joy.

When I was a boy I used to love Palm Sunday. One of the
things I remember is the great songs of praise and the
word "Alleluia" that we sing on this Sunday and next
Sunday. But before I spend all my time talking to you
about things I remember, I had better get to our story
for today. We are going to talk about some important
people. [**Hold up card reading "Richard Nixon".**] Who is
this person? Right, the President of the United States.
Would you say that he is a very important person? I
should say so. Who has ever heard of this one? [**Joe
Namath.**] Right, a champion football player. How about
this one? [**Fred Flintstone.**] Oh, everyone knows our
favorite cartoon character, Mr. Flintstone. [**Continue
holding up the rest of the name cards and discussing the
importance of each person in his field.**]

25

Say, everyone knew the last two names, my name and Janie's name. We must be getting more famous as we go along. You see, some names are so well known that all we have to do is see them or hear them and we can all say that we know them. It is nice when we can think that some of the names are people we know, and then we can call them our friends.

Let's take the names that we have talked about and put them on the board. I want you to tell me who is the most important person and I will put that name at the top. It surely is a fine list of names, and a list that you can be proud of knowing. You know what, though? I am going to ask you a very hard question because I don't think that we have really finished our list. There is one name I think of whenever I make a list of important people. This name is the most famous name of all time. Can anyone think of whom I am thinking of? JESUS, that's right, the most important name of all. The Bible teaches us that his name is so important that when it is mentioned it should be above every other name. The reason that this is so is because God was so pleased with what Jesus did that God made his name known to everyone in every time. What do you think we should do with the name JESUS?

Let's take his name and put it at the top of the list so that whenever anyone thinks of famous people or sees our list he will know who we think is the most important. That will show everyone who we believe is the most wonderful and most famous person in the whole world for all times.

A NEW LIFE

I Corinthians 15:20-26, verse 22: For as in Adam all die, so also in Christ shall all be made alive.

Object: Some egg shells and some baby chicks. These can be purchased at many stores at this time of the year.

Good morning, boys and girls. How are you today? This is the most wonderful day in our lives, Easter day. There is nothing like Easter for certain and wonderful excitement. Just think, almost two thousand years ago something took place that changed the entire world. Ever since that first Easter things have been different and men have looked forward to something called death that they used to be afraid of. But I am getting ahead of my story. I have something with me today that I have always wanted to share with you but have never had the opportunity before.

Look what I brought with me this morning. Eggs! Wonderful, beautiful eggs. Did a lot of you find eggs this morning when you got up? Were they colored in many beautiful ways? Good. Now I brought some plain eggs with me this morning and I want to tell you that they are dead. Yes, sir, I brought you nothing but some broken egg shells and they are dead. Look at that poor old egg shell and see how it is kind of cracked and uneven. The poor thing would have made someone a good breakfast, but the only thing that is left is a cracked, uneven, kind of pale white egg shell.

Now you know this egg shell reminds me of Jesus when he came down from the cross. He probably did not look much like he did when he was walking around the hills near Jerusalem or by the Sea of Galilee. He was dead. His skin was broken and bleeding. He was a different person to look at than the one you and I like to remember. But do you know what? Something exciting happened during the next couple of days after Jesus was taken down from the cross. It's the reason for Easter; it is the thing that makes Easter so exciting and wonderful. When the people went up to the place where Jesus had been buried they found the old tomb cracked open. When they looked inside it was as empty as the inside of this egg shell. That's right. The place where Jesus was supposed to be was empty except for some of the special clothes that they used to bury people in. And when they asked what had happened, an angel told them that he had risen from the dead.

One of the best ways I have to show you what I am talking about is a special little gift that I have for you. Do you remember what I said about this egg? It is now empty and it is cracked open. Well, what do you think was inside this egg before it cracked open? That's right, some of you guessed. A baby chicken. I am going to bring a couple out to show you right now what happened to the egg that died, and then after the service if your parents agree, I will give everyone a baby chick.

Do you see what happened? The egg had to first die inside so that it could become a chicken. It had to stop being an egg if it wanted to be a chicken. Someday you and I have to stop living the way that we are and die. When we die God promises us that we will become something brand new. We will become a new person as God wants us to be. We will not become a baby chick, but we will become someone like Jesus was after he came back from the tomb. Now you know why people were so happy when Jesus came back from the dead. They knew that they never had to worry about dying again. They knew that Jesus and God would bring them back to life. Isn't that wonderful? Now we know that we have a brand new life as a special gift from God.

THREE WITNESSES

I John 5:4-12, verse 8: There are three witnesses: the Spirit, the water and the blood; and these three agree.

Object: A dishpan, a dishcloth and a dishtowel.

Good morning to you. How are you on this beautiful day? Isn't it great to feel the warm sunshine of spring and to know that the good summer days are not very far away? It's nice to have winter when it starts and it's nice also to have it end. Speaking of end, do you know what we put on the end of all our prayers and many hymns? The word is **Amen.** Do you know what it means? It means "so be it."Amen, so be it, means we pray that what we have said will find favor with God and that we will be as He wants us to be.

That was a good thing to learn, wasn't it? Let me show you something else that we don't always understand but is very important to know. The Bible says there are three witnesses, the Spirit, the water and the blood. These three witnesses say that Jesus is the Son of God. Why are there three witnesses, and what are witnesses? I have brought some of my friends with me again this morning and I hope they will help us understand.

First of all I brought my friend, Davey Dishpan. Davey can hold water, but he can also hold vegetables to be cleaned. I also have another friend by the name of Debbie Dishtowel. With Debbie you can dry dishes, or dry your hands, or when she gets a little older you can even polish the furniture with her. One other friend is here today and his name is Dale Dishcloth. Dale will work hard for you when you tell him what to do. I have seen Dale wash dishes, clean off the table we eat on and wipe off the stove and refrigerator. Now my three friends can do lots of different things, but they do one very special job when they are all together. Do you know what they do best? That's right, they do the dishes. A dishpan, a dishcloth and a dishtowel all tell us that when they are used together there are some dirty dishes to be cleaned.

The person of Jesus was many things. When Jesus was baptized with **water,** God said that this was His beloved Son in whom He was well pleased. When Jesus died on the cross and the **blood** ran from his wounds, God said this was His Son in whom He was well pleased. And when St. Paul was on the road to Damascus he heard the **Spirit** of God tell him that Jesus was the Savior, the Son of God. God says that these are the three witnesses that Jesus is the Son.

Now Jesus was a very good teacher, and the things that he taught us we remember today. Jesus was a good doctor, a healer. The people he healed thought he performed miracles. Jesus was a great preacher, so great that we still remember his sermons from thousands of years ago. Jesus did everything well, but the witnesses tell us that he was even more than any of those things. The witnesses of the Spirit, the water and the blood tell us that he is the Christ, the Son of the living God.

Just as Davey, Debbie and Dale tell us that there are dishes to wash, so do the witnesses of the water, blood and Spirit tell us that Jesus is the Son of God and that we should worship him.

SUFFERING SOAPSUDS!

I Peter 2:11-20, verse 20: But if when you do right and suffer for it, you take it patiently, you have God's approval.

Object: Detergent used for washing clothes or dishes and a jar of hot water.

Good morning, boys and girls. A few days ago a little boy asked me if I had ever heard of the Dead Sea. When I said yes, he wanted to know what had made it sick and how it died. That is a very interesting question. The Dead Sea is in the Holy Land and it is the lowest spot on earth. In the water there is a lot of salt, just as there is in the ocean, but the water in the Dead Sea has nowhere to go and the Sea just gets saltier and saltier until nothing at all can live in it. There is not one living plant or one living fish and if you put one in the Dead Sea it would soon die. That is why it is called the Dead Sea.

I have some water in this jar to tell you a story about God. It is not from the Dead Sea, but I think that you will enjoy hearing what it tells us about God. Water is good, and we need it to live. Nothing can grow without water. We clean things with water, including ourselves. But sometimes things get so dirty and so messy that we cannot get them clean without giving the water a little help. Let me show you what I mean.

I brought with me this morning some soap that we use to wash our clothes or dishes. Now if I just take the soap out and smear it on a dirty plate I will not get the plate clean. It needs to be mixed with water. So let me put the detergent in the water and see what happens. Hmmm, nothing is happening. I wonder what is wrong. I thought that when I put the soap into the water it would turn into suds and then we could see what we use to wash. Does anyone know what to do so that I can have a lot of suds? [**Wait for suggestions.**] Shake the jar with the water and soap? Won't that hurt the water and the soap? I mean, how would you like it if I shook you? It doesn't feel very good to be shaken, does it? Well, we have to if we are going to have suds. [**Shake the jar vigorously.**] Wow, that really makes the suds. I see that you have to shake the jar or stir it up real hard if you're going to have good suds.

You know, that does make sense. That's the way it is in life. Sometimes we have to do things that aren't always a lot of fun in order to have things better later on. Which would you rather do, study hard or play? Which will you do if you want to grow up knowing something?' Dads must go to work when they would rather be home with you. They have to work if you're going to be able to eat and have new clothes. Jesus tells us through his disciples that sometimes we have to be patient and even suffer a little if we want God's approval later on. We have to be like the soap that needs to be shaken up real hard if it's ever going to amount to much. If we're going to be servants of Christ we have to suffer a little, be patient a lot and do it with lots of good humor rather than complaining.

Suffering helps to make us better people later on, even if it doesn't seem very kind or good now. Some people might think that water all by itself will get things clean, or that soap all by itself will do the same thing. But in the end, the soapsuds that you get by shaking the two up together are much better. If you think that things are sometimes too hard or if you get a hurt, just remember what had to happen to the soap before it could become better. Then you will perhaps know why God has allowed you to suffer or hurt for a little while. When you grow a little older you will be better because of it.

GOD DOESN'T CHANGE

James 1:17-21, verse 17: Every good endowment and every perfect gift is from above, coming down from the Father of lights with whom there is no variation or shadow due to change.

Object: A picture of yourself as a child and a loudly ticking clock [or a bright but constant light]

This morning, boys and girls, I'm going to try answering a question many of you have asked. People say to me, "Why is church almost always the same?" In some churches they sing the same songs every Sunday, they pray the same prayers and use the same faces, like those of the minister and the organist and the choir. Perhaps the answer is that once you have the best, why change? But that would not be right, because we all know that everything we do can stand improvement. Then why not change? Would God be angry if we changed? No, God would not be angry because God doesn't get angry. I think the best answer we have is that we all like to do things we do well, and we all like things that are familiar. For instance, did you know that one of the prayers that is prayed in almost every church is the same one Jesus taught his disciples almost two thousand years ago? And did you know that some of the hymns we sing are hymns that were sung when Jesus was brought to the Temple as a baby, or by Mary when she found out that she was going to have the baby Jesus? You don't want to forget things like that, so you sing and pray them over and over.

Does God change? Is God different today than He was yesterday? I have a picture here of a very good-looking boy. Do any of you know who this strong, handsome young man is? [**Let them guess.**] You probably won't believe it, but that young man is me when I was a boy.

Isn't is amazing how people change? Have you ever looked at pictures of yourself as a baby and then looked in a mirror to see how much you've changed? How about a seed? Does it change? I'll say it does.

But how about God? Does He change or does He stay the same? The Bible says God is unchanging, that He is the same today as He was yesterday and He will be the same tomorrow. Now you say that everything changes and you are just about right.Here's a clock that runs the same as any clock. Listen to it tick. It sounds almost the same every time. It sounds so much the same that I can't tell the difference between ticks. And here is a flashlight. When I turn it on the light stays the same. I can't tell whether it gets lighter or darker. These things seem the same. We might say that God is like the tick-tock of a clock or the light of a flashlight. God doesn't change because He is God and His love is the same for everybody. His rain and sunshine are the same for everybody. It doesn't make any difference if you lived a hundred years ago or right now, there would be the same God for you then as there is now.

I told you that the clock and the light are almost like God. But you and I know that sometimes a watch runs fast and sometimes a watch runs slow and sometimes if it isn't wound at the right time it will stop running. We also know that when I put new batteries in my flashlight the light is brighter than after I have used it for awhile and I know that in time it will stop burning altogether. But maybe it helps you to understand that there are some things we don't want to change and the most important of these is God. We would like to have a watch that always kept good time and never ran fast or slow or quit. And we would like to have a flashlight that never burned out. But most of all we want a God who will remain the **same for us** and for all people for all time.

34

TURNING ON THE LIGHTS

I Peter 2:21b-25, verse 25: For you were straying like sheep, but have returned to the Shepherd and Guardian of your souls.

Object: A light switch.

Good morning, boys and girls. How are you on this light and cheery day? Do any of you remember the days in the cold winter when it was still dark as you got up to come to church? Light is very important to us for a lot of reasons, isn't it? It is very hard to do many things in the dark. Have any of you tried to play games in the dark, or have you tried to read or eat without light? It isn't very easy, is it? On the altar of almost every church is something that tells us how important light is in our world. Have you ever asked the question, "Why do we have candles on our altar and why do we burn them even when we have the lights on?" I know that you have noticed the candles and have thought how beautiful they are. Have you ever heard someone talk about Jesus as the light of the world? That's what Jesus called himself, and Christians for thousands of years have been lighting candles to remember that Jesus showed us what God is. We don't have to wonder whether He loves us anymore. Before Jesus came we just had to guess a lot about God, and then we were kind of "in the dark." Not anymore! Jesus gave us light, so we remember him with candles.

Let me show you another way to think about it. I have something here with me this morning that all of you have seen before. You probably have more than one in many of the rooms in your house. [**Hold up light switch and let them guess what it is.**] That is right, a light switch. I don't suppose that we think much about light switches because when we walk into the room we give a flick or a turn and the lights come on. But have you ever been in a dark room where you did not know where the light switch was? I remember when I was little I used to be afraid in the dark. I would have to ask my mother or father to go with me to the room until I could have the lights turned on. That old light switch always felt so good to my fingers because I knew when I touched it the lights would come on as fast as I flicked it. Without the light switch I felt lost and afraid.

That's the way Jesus is to Christians. When Jesus is near there is never any fear. Peter, in his letter to some Christian people, said that before they became Christians they were like sheep who were just wandering around, not knowing where they were going, always getting lost and separated from other sheep. But since they knew Jesus, who was like a shepherd, they were not afraid because they were not alone. The Bible uses another word to tell us how important Jesus is to us. The word is guardian. That means someone who looks after us as though we were all children, even your fathers and mothers. Just as you want your mother and dad to go with you into a dark room and turn on the lights, so Jesus is our guardian and goes with our whole family wherever we go and watches out for us so that we will have nothing to fear.

It is easy to turn on the lights when we have a light switch. And it's easy to know how much God loves us when we have Jesus. The next time you see a light switch you can remember this: Jesus is like a light switch because he brings understanding about God just as the light switch brings light into the dark room. Once you were afraid of dark rooms, but not anymore, because you now can turn on the lights and see everything. People used to be afraid of God because they had never known what God was like. But now they know since they have Jesus.

LISTENING AND DOING

James 1:22-27, verse 23: For if anyone is a hearer of the word and not a doer, he is like a man who observes his natural face in a mirror, for he observes himself and goes away and at once forgets what he was like.

Object: A snapshot or several snapshots of people or places..

Good morning, boys and girls. It's good to see you after a whole week of not being together. Do you ever forget what I look like when you don't see me for seven days? People like to think they know and can remember faces, but sometimes it is hard. How many of you remember or think you know what Jesus looked like when he lived in Nazareth and other parts of Israel? You do? [**Hold up a familiar picture of Jesus.**] Is this what he looked like as you remember him?

How many of you think you could tell me what you look like to other people? [**Ask a couple and repeat what they say.**] It is hard to tell others what you look like unless you have a mirror or maybe a picture of yourself to describe. Last summer when I was on vacation I visited some beautiful places, so beautiful that I wanted to make sure that I would never forget them. Do you know what I did? [**Let them reply.**] That's right, I took pictures and I brought some of them along this morning. It's good that I have these pictures, too, because I couldn't remember who else was with us until I looked at the picture. When I look I see how tall the trees are, so big they won't fit into the picture. Look at how green the grass was. Do you see my old friend, Danny, my dog? It surely is good that I take pictures, because I will be able to remember that vacation for many years with their help.

There is a good lesson to learn about how God teaches us what is right and wrong, what to believe and what not to believe. God wants us to listen to what He says. God likes good listeners who pay attention, but He also wants the hearers to **do** what He says. If we just listen, God says, and don't do what He tells us to do, then we will soon forget. Just as I would have forgotten about my vacation if I had not taken those beautiful pictures, so I forget about what God tells me if I don't work at it.

Suppose God says, "Forgive those who hate you." If I say, "That's good, I will forgive Mike for hitting me," but then I never forgive Mike, I quickly forget that God has spoken to me. So God wants us to do good things as well as hear good things because it helps to make us better people and helps other people to get to know about God through us.

Just remember how easy it is to forget -- so easy that it is hard to remember things just last summer. That is, unless you have a picture to help you. So when God speaks to you remember that most of the time He wants you to do two things and not just one. Listen, that's first; and second, **do** what He has told you.

LOVE COVERS UP OUR SINS

I Peter 4:7b-11, verse 8: Above all, hold unfailing your love for one another, since love covers a multitude of sins.

Object: An old shoe and some shoe polish.

Good morning, boys and girls. Isn't this a beautiful morning? I don't suppose that very many of you walked to church this morning, did you? A long time ago the only way that people went anywhere was by walking. There are some places in the world today that you can only reach by walking. In the Holy Land most of the people still walk and they still wear the same kind of shoes in many places that Jesus wore when he lived there. How many of you know what kind of shoes Jesus wore when he lived on earth? That's right, sandals. Do any of you wear sandals in the summertime? A lot of you do.

I brought along with me this morning one of my old shoes. While it isn't a sandal, it sure does look like it has been walking on a lot of dusty roads, just like the ones in the Holy Land. This poor old shoe looks like it has seen better days. Who wants a shoe that looks as bad as this one does? The only place for this shoe is in the garbage can. It's really bad. You know what this shoe reminds me of? It reminds me of some people I know. That's right, people. Have you ever known some people who never seem to do anything right? They always do the wrong thing. Before long these people start to look bad as well as do bad. They are like my shoe, for they get all scuffed up and look dirty and pretty soon these people look like they belong on a junk pile.

What can you do with a pair of shoes that looks this bad if

39

you don't want to throw them away? What do you do with your shoes when they look that bad? [**See if anyone will answer that they can be shined.**] That's right, you shine your shoes when they get muddy or scuffed. Do you think that will work with my shoe? I just happen to have some polish and a rag with me this morning and we could try to see if it helps. [**Begin to shine the shoes and finish the sermon while you are doing so.**] We could pretend that these scuffs and dirty marks are sins that you and I do everyday to each other. Do you know what I mean? The time you said something not very nice about one of your friends, or told a lie, or maybe when you used God's name in the wrong way. We call those things sins. That's bad, and look what it does to us. It makes marks on us just as the dirt makes marks on the shoes. But you know, God said that there is one thing that covers up our sins. That one thing is love. Let's pretend that the shoe polish is like love and see what happens to our marked-up shoes. When we try to do things in love then we don't do those things that hurt other people like lying or saying bad words.

Now let's see what our love did to this person or what the polish did to the shoe. Oh, my, it is beautiful again! If shoe polish can do this to shoes, just think what love does to human beings. If this old shoe can be made to look this good, then some of those sad, tired, unhappy people whom we thought should be put on the human junkpile can be made to look and feel brand new again also.

ASKING IN JESUS' NAME

I John 16:23b-30, verse 24: Hitherto you have asked nothing in my name, ask and you will receive, that your joy may be full.

Object: Things that identify a name: tongue depressor -- doctor; money changer or newpaper bag -- paper boy; stole -- pastor; policeman's badge -- policeman, etc.

Wouldn't it be wonderful if some morning I said, "Good morning" to everyone and used your names? Good morning, Carol; Good morning, John, etc. But we never seem to have enough time. Names are important. Do you know what the name **Jesus** means? There used to be a lot of people who had the name Jesus, but there are few anymore. A long time ago people used the name as they use John or James today, and then they would very often tell who the father was or what town the person was from. For instance, they called Jesus "Jesus, son of Joseph," and "Jesus of Nazareth." Jesus means "God's salvation," which is exactly what he means to us.

Sometimes all we have to do is see something and right away we think of somebody or what he does. For instance, if I took this piece of wood and asked you to open your mouth wide, who would you think of right away? [**Let them answer.**] Very good, a doctor. How about this one? [**Newspaper bag.**] Right! When you see one of these you immediately think of a person who uses **policeman's badge.**] Right again. When you see one of these things you immediately think of a person who uses it and that reminds you of someone's name like Dr. Jones or newsboy John or Patrolman McCarthy.

There is something else to think about also. If you need a

41

newspaper to read, you don't go to the doctor, do you? Of course not. You would say, "John, I want a newspaper. Can you help me?" And he would. He would see that you got the paper you wanted. That's what Jesus wants you and me to do with him. Jesus says that when we have somethng to ask of God, whether it be for his help, his love, or peace, we should ask it in Jesus' name and we will get it. You can't read John the newsboy, but John will get the newspaper for you to read. Well, Jesus isn't medicine, but he can help you when you are sick to get the right medicine. And Jesus isn't a road sign, but he can help you when you feel lost.

Do you understand what I mean? If you need something, ask God in the name of Jesus and He will see that what is best for you will happen. And don't forget his name: we call him Jesus, which means "God's salvation." Jesus is God's way of helping us when we are in need.

PROBLEMS AND ANSWERS

Romans 11:33-36, verse 33: O the depth of the riches and wisdom and knowledge of God! How unsearchable are his judgments and how inscrutable his ways!

Object: A tough math problem with all sorts of signs, numbers and letters.

Good morning, boys and girls. Welcome to the house of the richest person in the world. Did you know that? Who lives in this house whom we call the richest person in the whole world? [**Let them answer.**] That's right, this is God's House. Why do we say that He is rich? Does God have money, or jewels, or gold? Well, in a way He does and in a way He doesn't. God owns everything and He just lends it to us to use while we live here on the good earth. That's one reason why we should take such good care of everything that we have, because God gives it to us.

But God is more than rich. He is smart, too. Let me show you what I mean. How many of you like arithmetic? Some of you do. Who thinks he can work any problem? [**Choose a volunteer.**] Now let's see how good you are. How much is two plus two? [**Go on giving some quick, easy questions that they will all know.**] That's very good. Now try this one. [**Bring out the board with the big problem.**] Can you give me the answer to that one? Maybe you need a few minutes to work on it. We'll let you study the problem while we talk.

Sometimes, boys and girls, we have problems that are hard ones to figure out. We wonder why some people are rich and others are poor, why some people are healthy and some are sick, and why some are real smart and others have a hard time learning to read. What are the answers? Nobody I know has the answers to such difficult problems. Then we think that maybe there are no answers.

Let's check with our arithmetic expert and see how he is doing. How are you coming with the problem? Do you have the answer? No? Do you think there is an answer? Somebody knows how to work it, but you don't.

Well, that's what I have been trying to tell the other boys and girls about people problems. We have problems, but the answers are beyond us. Who knows the answers to our problems as people? It's not other people. Who is it then? That's right, God. Only God knows all of the answers and we are like —————— who tried to work the hard problem. There is an answer but it is beyond us.

So God is not only rich, but He is also very smart, so smart that He knows all of the answers to every problem we will ever have.

FILLED WITH GOD'S SPIRIT

Acts 2:1-11, verse 4: And they were all filled with the Holy Spirit and began to speak in other tongues, as the Spirit gave them utterance.

Object: Some large containers with things to fill them: trash,candy, clothes, empty bottles, etc.

Good morning to you and welcome to God's House. It really makes everyone feel good when God's house is filled and it makes us sad when it isn't filled. Jesus used to tell stories about how God wanted His Kingdom filled with people who wanted to believe and be a part of Him. Once he told a story about a great dinner that a king had prepared. The king invited all of his friends. But his friends made excuses and told the king that they couldn't come. Well, the king just sent his helpers out to find strangers so that his house would be filled by those who wanted to eat the good food. God always wants His church filled whenever there are services.

Let me show you something. Do you see this big basket? What do you do with a basket? Do you just carry it around? No, you fill it. Now the basket can be filled with lots of things. For instance, here are some clothes.Let's see if we can fill the basket with clothes. Sure we can.The basket will also take food, or it will even take trash. You see, a basket needs to be filled.

A long time ago the disciples of Jesus were sitting in a room when they heard a noise like a great wind and they ran outside: The disciples felt kind of empty and sad because Jesus was not living with them as he had for a couple of years. But when they ran outside, something wonderful happened -- so wonderful that they never forgot. They were filled with the Holy Spirit, the Spirit of God. This Spirit filled them up just like our basket was filled, and they received great strength and wisdom.

The same thing happens to all of us in one way or another. We are all empty until we are filled with something. We can be filled with hate and anger, or we can be filled with joy and love. When we have joy and love then we know that our prayer that God would fill us has been answered.

SHARING OURSELVES

I John 3:13-18, verse 17: But if anyone has the world's goods and sees his brother in need, yet closes his heart against him, how does God's love abide in him?

Object: A six-foot measuring tape.

Good morning, boys and girls. How are you this Memorial Day weekend? Memorial Day is an important day in our country because we remember all the people who shared their lives and died so that our country would be just the kind of country we want it to be. Our country is a little sad because so many men had to die in war to keep us free, but we are also very grateful.

God teaches us to share everything including our lives. I want to show you what I mean. Here is something that a carpenter uses. It is also something that children love to play with when they can get ahold of it. Do you know what this is? [**Let them guess.**] That's right, it is a measuring tape. Measuring tapes aren't only fun but also very useful. For instance, if I want to know how far it is from here [**mark a spot**] to here [**mark a spot**], I just have to measure it. But suppose my measuring tape doesn't want to share itself with me? I can stand here and yell and scream, or I can say "pretty please," but if the measuring tape doesn't want to come out of its case I can't measure the distance. Of course, the tape isn't much good just staying in there all by itself. As a matter of fact, it is nothing but a big blob until it does share itself.

Well, let's see how we can do this. You [**choose a volunteer**] mark this spot and you [**choose another**] mark this one. Fine. I'll stretch out the tape so we can see how

47

far it is from here to there. It's exactly four feet and three inches long. How great it is when the tape measure shares itself with us.

That's just the way it is with people. If you don't share yourself with other people, giving them the things that you have, you are just a big blob. This is also the way we know that you don't let God's love into your heart. For if you let God's love into your heart then you will share everything that you have with others.

So remember, you can be like a measuring tape. You can be a selfish blob **without** God, or a generous, loving, sharing person **with** God.

PASSING WITH FLYING COLORS!

I John 3:13-18, verse 14: We know that we have passed out of death into life because we love the brethren.

Object: A report card with all passing grades on it.

Good morning, boys and girls. Welcome to the first Sunday in June. This is the sixth month of the year and when it is over the first half of the year will have passed. But June is a good month for another reason, isn't it? How many of you have just finished school? Isn't it great to have a month like June to begin your vacation from school? Is there anyone who went to school who doesn't know what I have in my hand? [**Hold up a report card.**] Yes, sir, this is a report card. Sometimes we like these things and sometimes we don't. It tells us how we have done, whether we paid attention to what the teacher taught us and what kinds of habits we have, like not talking when we are supposd to be quiet and how we treat our friends.

Let's look at this report card and see how I did during the year. Let's see, I got an A in reading and a B in spelling and a C in arithmetic. Well, that's not too bad, although I could have done better if I had tried harder. Let's see what else my report card says. It tells me that I attended every day except twice and that was when I was sick. And I was not late one time.

Oh, there is one other thing that my report card tells me at the end of the year. When it's all over it tells me whether I passed or failed. Let's see what it says, Oh, boy, I passed and next year I will be in the fourth grade!

It means a lot to know that I have passed.That's the way

Jesus wants us to feel, too. He spoke to his disciple, John, and told him that someday everybody who loved God would pass into a new world, God's new world.

That's kind of the way it is when we die here on earth. When we die Jesus says we are passed into a new life in heaven. Not many of you ever thought that dying could be so wonderful, did you? But it is. Someday we will be passed into heaven just as we pass into the next grade at school How do we pass? We pass by loving God and all the people in the world.

So remember, what is dying like? It is like passing a grade in school We all know how happy that experience is, don't we?

50

WE ARE LIKE CLAY

I Peter 5:6-11, verse 6: Humble yourselves therefore under the mighty hand of God, that in due time he may exhalt you.

Object: Clay or crazy putty. You may find some in your Sunday School nursery.

Good morning, boys and girls. How are you on this lovely God's day? Isn't it wonderful the way God made the world and then put all sorts of things in it? Do you know when I was a little boy I used to love to make things out of a special material called clay? How many of you have ever worked with clay? Isn't it fun? I think so, too.

But have you ever really looked at clay? [**Show them the clay.**] It's just a big gray blob. That's right. There is nothing very pretty about a lumpy old piece of gray clay. As a matter of fact, to look at that lumpy, old, slimy gray piece of clay kind of makes you feel sorry for it. Poor old clay. What good is anything that looks like this? I'm sure I don't know.

On the other hand, if you pick that piece of clay up in your hands and begin to roll it and twist it and make it soft and workable, you can do a lot of things with it. Men have made statues that look so real they remind you of people. Some others have made flowers and trees out of clay and after they were painted they looked almost as beautiful as a real flower and tree. [**You might press the clay against something to show how an image can be made in the clay.**]

Well, you know, boys and girls, we are like that clay in the sight of God. If God just left us alone and never cared for us or loved us, we would not be very pretty or strong or happy. If God just left us alone we would look like that lump of clay before we worked with it. Now, who wants to be like an old lump of clay when we can look as beautiful as a flower or as strong as a tree? So remember who it is who makes you what you are. It's God! God loves you and can fill you full of love. God cares for you and you care about others.

It's nice to know that God thinks so much about us that we never have to worry about being old lumps of clay. He will make us into something that He needs and something that we will want to be.

WAITING AND WORKING FOR GOD

Romans 8:18-23, verse 19: For all creation is waiting patiently and hopefully for that future day when God will glorify his children.

Object: A calendar.

Good morning, boys and girls. How are you today? Did you know that this is the end of the third week in June, the first day of the week, the sixth month of the year? That's right. Do you know how I know all of that? **[Let them guess.]** I'll show you how. **[Bring out the calendar.]**

That's right, a calendar. It is pretty important. Let's see what we can find out with a calendar. What is your favorite holiday? **[Wait for the answer: Christmas, Fourth of July, Halloween. . .]** When is Christmas? December 25. **[Look up the date and give the day and the week.]** Let's see about another day, like your birthday. **[Look up several birthdays.]** Some people have to wait a long time for their birthdays, while others will have a birthday very soon. All of us have to wait together for Christmas and New Year's and Valentine's Day. But there is nothing that we can do except wait. If we paced up and down, would that special day come any sooner? Or if we were to wring our hands or jump up and down would that day say, "Oh, let's hurry up so that Mike or Sally or Peter won't have to wait so long?" Of course we know that would not happen.

That's the way it is with God and His world. A lot of people walk around worrying about when God is going to make this world come to an end and start a new one. But worrying about that doesn't do a bit of good. These things happen only when God wants them to and not any sooner.

But I want to tell you something that I **do** know that is very important. While we are waiting for God's very special time, just as when we are waiting for our birthdays or Christmas or Halloween, we have a lot of time to do good for other people. And you know what? When God builds His new world with heavens and earth, He will find a special place for you in it. Won't that be great? So fill your calendar with good days, doing good things and when the time is just right God will surprise you with His new world.

HOW WE USE OUR TONGUES

I Peter 3:8-15a, verse 10: If you want a happy, good life, keep control of your tongue, and guard your lips from telling lies.

Object: A shoe tongue and a wagon tongue.

Good morning, boys and girls. This is the last Sunday in June and we wonder where the days have gone. Have you ever noticed how the same word is used for different things? For instance, the word "hair" can be something that grows on your head, or it can be a rabbit (hare.) And the word "sea" can be an ocean or the way to look at something (see).

I brought along a couple of things that are called by the same name but are not alike. [**Bring out the wagon and shoe.**] Did you know that both the shoe and wagon have a part that has the same name. That's right. They both have tongues. Can you believe that they have tongues? Well, they do. Let me show you. [**Show them both parts.**] Now the tongue on the wagon is very important because that is how you steer it. Whichever way you pull the tongue the wagon has to go. The tongue in the shoe is very important also for it keeps your shoe laces from hurting your feet. These tongues are very important.

There is another tongue that you know a lot about, don't you? Where is your tongue? In your mouth, that's right. And, oh, how important it is. That tongue can help you do all sorts of things. If you are not careful it can get you into trouble. Sometimes we say things that we are sorry for and wish that we had not said, and then we kind of get angry at our tongues.

But our tongues also help us to pray and sing and say kind things. With our tongues we can say, "I love you" or we can say "God bless our mothers and fathers." A tongue is important, and a tongue in our mouth is the most important tongue of all.

So remember when you see a wagon or when you put on a shoe that they have tongues that are pretty important. Then you will say, "I have a tongue that is even more important than yours, Mrs. Wagon and Miss Shoe. And God wants me to treat it right and only do good with it." Your tongue is God's tongue to tell others about Jesus.

UNITED WITH JESUS

Romans 6:3-11, verse 5: For if we have been united with him in a death like his, we shall certainly be united with him in a resurrection like his.

Object: An American flag.

Good morning, boys and girls. How are you on this great day? Do you know what special day comes around this time of the year? That's right, the Fourth of July. Do you know why we have a celebration on the Fourth of July? [**Let them answer.**] That is when our forefathers told the whole world that we were going to take care of ourselves. A Declaration of Independence was signed.

Here is a hard question. Do you know what the symbol of our country is? [**Wait for answer, the flag.**] I brought a flag with me today to see if you can tell me what it means. We know that it is red, white and blue, but do you know what the stars stand for on this field of blue? They represent the states, so how many are there? Fifty! That's right. One of the stars is for Ohio and another for California and one for Florida and another for Maine. All fifty states are represented here and they are called the United States. Fifty states make one whole country. We are **UNITED** and that means we belong to each other.

That isn't all that we are united with though. We belong to someone else besides people in other states. The Bible teaches us that when we are baptized we are united with Jesus in his death. We are a part of his dying. Because we are ready to die with Jesus we are also going to be united with him in the resurrection. Let me tell you what that means. It means that we are all going to die just as Jesus died, maybe not in the same way, but we are going to die. But Jesus came back from death and lived again. Now he lives forever and so will we. Because we believe in Jesus we are united with him and whatever happened to him is going to happen to us because we belong to each other, just like the states in the United States are part of each other.

Isn't it wonderful that we are going to spend forever with Jesus? I think so!

WHO DO YOU BELONG TO?

Romans 6:19-23, verse 22: But now you are free from the power of sin and are slaves of God, and his benefits to you include holiness and everlasting life.

Object: Handcuffs, cuff links with initial.

Good morning, boys and girls. How are you today? Isn't this a wonderful time of the year? Each day when you get up you can go outside and play and do whatever you want to do. Some people can't, you know.

Let me show you what I have with me today. [**Bring out handcuffs.**] What are these? That's right, handcuffs. The policeman has handcuffs. He has them to put on people who don't obey the law. When the policeman catches the crook he puts handcuffs on him and the crook belongs to him. The crook doesn't like the policeman and the policeman doesn't like the crook, but they belong to each other because of the handcuffs.

That's the way sin is to us. When we commit sins we belong to whatever is wrong. We don't like the sin and it probably is not very kind to us, but we are together because we belong to each other.

Here is another thing that we wear on our wrists called a cuff link. This is a special cuff link and it also tells me that I belong. Do you see this initial, the letter "R"? That stands for my last name and it means that I belong to all of my family. I belong to my mother and father, my brothers and sisters, my wife and my children and everyone who is in my family.

I also can belong to God in the same way. There are

things that I want to do because God made me a part of His family. When I belong to Him I try not to sin or to hurt others, but instead I want to be a part of His love.

You have a choice of what kind of thing you will want on your wrist -- handcuffs or cuff links. You can also belong to God and His love or to evil and its sin. But one thing is certain: You must belong to one or the other. Either you belong to evil and sin or to God and His love.

PAIRING UP WITH GOD

Romans 8:12-17, verse 14: For all who are led by the Spirit of God are sons of God.

Object: Bottle caps and bottles, salt and pepper shakers, cup and saucer --any paired items.

Good morning to you, boys and girls. Have you ever noticed how some things just seem to go together? Let me see how smart you are this morning. I have brought a number of items with me and I want to see if a volunteer can help me find which things go together. Now I am going to lay them out here in front of you and you can all play the game with the volunteer secretly. [**Lay out each item on a big cloth with the things separated like the bottle cap and bottle, etc.**]

That's very good. You have put all the things back together the way they belong. God thinks of us in much the same way and knows that we go together with Him or with someone else. St. Paul learned from God that people who were led by the Spirit of God acted like sons of God. Let me explain this.

People who read their Bibles, attend services of worship, sing hymns and pray every day and who try to learn what God wants them to learn are going to be the sons of God. People who like to spend their time learning how to hate, fight, lie and cheat will not be like God. They will not be sons of God. People go together just as things do. Remember how you knew the bottle caps and bottles went together ? Well, so do people and the Spirit of God.

Wouldn't it be wonderful to be known as a son of God and

a brother to Jesus? It would, and you can be just that by following what the Spirit of God leads you to do.

PROBLEMS OLD AND NEW

I Corinthians 10:1-13, verse 13a: But remember this, the wrong desires that come into your life aren't new and different. Many others have faced exactly the same problems before you.

Object: Some old-fashioned glass rims and a pair of modern glasses; a horn that was used for the hard of hearing and a new hearing aid; a sprinkling can and a new yard sprinkler.

Good morning, boys and girls. I'm here to tell you hello for Jesus. That's right, Jesus has asked me to give you his greetings. One of the things that people wish would happen is that Jesus would be able to talk to them just as he talked to Peter or John or Mary. Some of us call that a problem. But it isn't a new problem any more than I suppose any other problem that we have is new.

Let me show you what I mean. Look what I have with me today. [**Hold up a pair of the latest style glasses.**] Many of you have seen these before. They are a pair of new eyeglasses. People who have a problem seeing wear glasses and it helps them solve their problem. Look at these old glasses that I have and you will see what I mean. They used to have problems with bad eyesight many years ago, too.

Or look at this old horn that people used to help them hear. Today we have a very powerful little box that allows people who have the same kind of problem to hear better than they could without any help.

Problems, problems, problems -- we all have problems

and people have always had problems. But God tells us that there is no problem so big that He can't help you solve it. Do you understand? We have problems called sins that have always been with us.They hurt us badly if we just let them alone. But God says to tell Him about your sins and He will help you find the answer and will give you the strength to overcome them.

Some people can't see very well so they wear glasses.Some people can't hear very well so they wear a hearing aid and it helps their problem. All of us have problems with our sins and God says, "I am the answer to help you overcome them."

GETTING THE FACTS

I Corinthians 15:1-10, verse 3: First and foremost, I handed on to you the facts which had been imparted to me; that Christ died for our sins, in accordance with the scriptures.

Object: A scale and some packages of different sizes and weights.

Good morning, children. How are you on this beautiful day? Have you ever played the game called "Telephone"? Someone whispers to you and you whisper it to someone else and by the time it gets to the end of the line it sounds very funny because it is different from when it was first said. That's the way rumors begin and what you hear may not always be true.

When St. Paul preached he hardly ever whispered and his preaching was always based on facts. Let me show you what I mean. I brought with me some packages this morning. Perhaps you can help me because I must take them to the Post Office and they always charge me according to how much my package weighs. How much do you think this one weighs? [**Hold up a package.**] Ten pounds, you say? O.K., how much does this one weigh? Five pounds. And this? Well, you might be pretty close. But you know that kind of weighing would never work. The Post Office makes me use one of these. [**Hold up scale.**] I must know exactly how much each package weighs. Let's just see how close you were. [**Weigh each package and compare.**] That's getting the facts. Two and one half pounds, one half pound and one pound. Those are the facts.

Well, that's the way Paul felt when he talked about

Jesus. He wanted to tell people the facts as they had been given to him. What are the facts? Paul says the facts are that Christ died for our sins; that he was raised from the dead on the third day; that Peter and the other disciples saw Jesus after the resurrection; then 500 people saw him at one time; then Jesus talked to James and finally even Paul met him.

Paul says that these are facts, not rumors or guesses. So just as you can be sure when you weigh something on the scale, you can also be sure about what Paul says about Jesus. Paul is like a good scale -- he gives us the facts.

THE BIG SPLASH!

2 Corinthians 3:4-9, verse 9: If splendor accompanied the dispensation under which we are condemned, how much richer in splendor must that one be under which we are acquitted!

Object: A stone and a piece of wood that floats [approximately the same size] and a bucket of water.

Good morning, boys and girls. How are you today? Isn't it wonderful to have the time to come and worship God and be together? I brought a couple of my friends with me again this morning. I don't know if you have ever met them before, so let me introduce you to them. Boys and girls, this is Wilbur Wood and Stanley Stone.

Now let me show you why my friends came with me today.Have you ever heard of someone making a "big splash"? That generally means that they have made some big news, really big news. You know, a long time ago Moses made a big splash when he came down from the mountain and told people all about receiving the ten commandments from God. Ths law told them all the things they had better not do, or they would end up in a pretty bad place. That was a really big splash! And the people really listened -- for awhile.

Jesus made a big splash, too, when he told the people why he had come. He said that he knew they were in trouble and he had just come to tell them that he was going to help them out of their trouble -- with love.

I don't know who made the bigger splash, but maybe

our friends can help. Now first I'm going to drop Stanley into the water. Stanley is like the Ten Commandments. Wow, that was some splash! Now we will try Wilbur. Wilbur is like love. Oh, that was good, but not quite as big a splash as Stanley. You might think that Stanley won, except for one thing: Stanley made a big splash and then went right to the bottom. But Wilbur Wood made a pretty big splash and now he is still floating around on the top of the water.

That's the way it is with the love of Jesus. It not only happens once, but it stays with you forever. Love is not just one big splash. It stays around for a long time, as long a time as you do and then even longer. That's what we like about Jesus' love -- it is with us forever.

JESUS' LASTING LOVE

Galatians 3:16-22, verse 19: It was a temporary measure pending the arrival of the issue to whom the promise was made. It was promulgated through angels and there was an intermediary.

Object: An arm cast or a crutch. [If you use the cast call the hospital and ask if they would make one for you.] Because you may not be able to obtain the cast, we shall do the lesson using the crutch as the object.

Good morning, boys and girls. Have you ever hurt your ankle or foot badly enough that you were not supposed to walk on it for a while? What did you do? Did you just lie down and stay there until it got better? You didn't? What **did** you do? Did you hop around on one leg or push a chair in front of you or lean on someone's shoulder?

I know what I would do if I hurt my leg and needed some help in this temporary situation. I would get some temporary help, like Clyde Crutch. Do you know what I mean when I say **temporary**? [**Let them answer.**] That's right, it means "for a little while." Clyde Crutch would help me walk for a little while or **temporarily** until my leg got better. Nothing wrong with Clyde. As a matter of fact, we need Clyde, but only until the leg is healed.

Well, Clyde is like God's law. We need the law to tell uswhen we are doing wrong or until we know Jesus. Jesus is love and where Clyde was only temporary, Jesus is permanent. We need Jesus forever. The law, like Clyde Crutch, is important when we are not living in love. But when we have the love of God we do more than the law even suggests. The law tells you that you must

69

respect other people. Jesus teaches us to love everyone, even those who are our enemies.

So remember, the law is like Clyde Crutch -- necessary, but only temporary. Jesus brings us love and it lasts forever.

Galatians 5:16-24 verse 16: I mean this: if you are guided by the Spirit you wil not fulfill the desires of your lower nature.

Object: A ruler or a circle compass and a Bible.

Good morning, boys and girls. How are you on this very last Sunday in August? It won't be very long before the summer vacation will be over and the new school year will begin again.

I just happen to have one of those things that is so important to anyone going to school. This is a very simple tool, but one that we use very often in our work and at school. We call this a ruler. We can measure the distance in the number of inches or we can do something else with it that is also very important to us at times. Do you know what else I can do with a ruler besides measure the number of inches that are between two points? [**See if you can get anyone to say "draw a straight line"**] That's right, I can draw a straight line with it. When I do that I call it a guide. The ruler is my guide to drawing a straight line. If I don't use the ruler and just try to draw a line, it soon becomes very crooked. But if I want to make it straight I just pick up the ruler, lay it down on the paper and make my pencil go right beside the ruler and I have a straight line.

We need those kinds of guides to draw and we need other kinds of guides to make sure our lives are lived the way God wants us to live. The Bible is a guide because it tells us how God lived in Jesus and what He said about living in this world.

71

As a matter of fact, the Spirit of God is a guide who tells us not only what **not** to do but also what to do. The Spirit of God is like a ruler because when we put our life next to his, we can't go any way except the right way. We need God to do this for us because if we don't have God we will soon wander all around and we will get into trouble.

So the next time you see a ruler you can remember that not only does it help you measure and draw straight lines, but it also reminds you that God is like a ruler because He guides us to live the good life.

SHARING THE LOAD

Galatians 5:25-6:10, verse 2: Help one another to carry these heavy loads, and in this way you will fulfill the law of Christ.

Object: A box of bricks or any heavy object that can be lifted by two.

Good morning to you, boys and girls. I wonder what has happened this week or is going to happen that is different from what you have been doing for the past several months? How many went back to school this week? How many have started for the first time? Isn't school fun, at least most of the time? What part of school do you like the best?

I know something about school that everyone likes. It is called sharing. The first thing that you get to share is yourself. Who do you share yourself with at school? The teacher, right, and the other boys and girls. Sharing is fun, and also very important. Even Jesus says that it is very important.

Let me show you what I mean. [**Select a volunteer and make sure that the group would think of this person as someone who is very strong.**] Now you can all see that I have selected a friend of yours who is pretty strong and should be able to handle this little assignment that I have for him. We want him to pick up this box that I have here and hold it for a few minutes while I talk to you. [**Give him the box.**]

You see the kind of thing that Jesus was talking about was not just big boxes, but he asked us to share our problems with each other as well. For instance, when one of our friends is sick we learn to send cards and maybe even give gifts so that the time will pass more quickly.

Let's see how our strong friend is doing. Is it getting pretty heavy? Would you like a little help? [**Select another child to help him hold it.**] That's a lot better, isn't it? Well, that is what Jesus meant when he told us to share the heavy loads, the big problems. So the next time you are sad, like maybe when a pet dies or you get hurt, talk it over with a friend and you will be glad that you did.

JESUS' TREASURE CHEST

Ephesians 3:13-21, verse 16: That out of the treasures of his glory he may grant you strength and power through his Spirit in your inner being.

Object: A treasure chest with the word Christ marked on it.

Good morning, boys and girls. Isn't this a beautiful day? There really is something special about Sunday and it is good that we keep it that way. I want to take you on a very special trip this morning because I found in my office a special map marked with a special sign. [**XR should be written on it.**] If we follow this map we may find a treasure at the place marked on the map. How many want to follow me to see what we can find?

I wonder what kind of a treasure you could find in a church. This map is marked with the symbols that mean Christ. [**When you have discovered the treasure chest you remark that the chest says Christ's Treasure on the outside.**] I wonder what kind of treasure Jesus must have in this special box. What would you think that Jesus would want to give us from his treasure? Gold, silver, money, jewels and precious things are what men would put in such a chest, but what would Jesus want to give us?

Some people think that his treasure chest doesn't have silver and gold and money because he doesn't have such things to give. But that isn't true, because it was God who made the gold and silver to begin with and put it in the ground for men to use. If Jesus thought that silver and gold were the most important he would have put them in there so that we could have them. What, then, would Jesus put in his treasure chest? Shall we open it and see? [**Open the treasure chest very carefully and take out either the words or symbols for the words like power and strength and peace and charity and love.**] My,

My, oh, my, you can sure tell what Jesus thinks is the most important thing, can't you? There isn't any silver or gold, but the things that are really important to God. That's why when you come to church or Sunday School the things that you learn about are not how to make money, but instead how to make friends with God and other people. So from now on we will remember what Jesus considers to be the real treasures of life, won't we?

LIVING TOGETHER IN PEACE

Ephesians 4:1-6, verse 3: Spare no effort to make fast with bonds of peace the unity which the Spirit gives.

Object: Name tags with the words "We try harder."

Isn't it great to get up on Sunday morning and have a place to go with the entire family where you can sing together, pray together, listen together and then visit with your friends again? I think so, and I hope you look forward to seeing me as much as I look forward to seeing you each Sunday.

Today I have something that I want to give you that you can wear all day long and perhaps a lot of times during the week. What I have for you must be explained so that you will understand why you are wearing it. Do you see this tag that I have here? It has some words printed on the tag that say, "We Try Harder." That is what I want to explain to you.

You know people have a hard time getting along with one another. I am sure that you have seen on your TV pictures of wars or trouble that sometimes happens in our cities or even fights that happen at school or sometimes in our own backyards. Why, I even heard the other day that some brothers and sisters fight with each other once in a while! That is only a rumor, but I hear that it really does happen once in a while. Well, St. Paul knew from all of his missionary journeys that people had a hard time getting along with each other, so he wrote a letter to some people in a town called Ephesus. He said that they should try harder to get along with each other because that is the way God wanted them to live. That's right, God said that He wants people to live in peace.

Well, that message is still true today.God wants people to live together and be happy. He doesn't want them to fight and make each other angry. Now who do you think He has asked to set the example in the world for the way He wants people to live? Christians! We are supposed to try harder than anyone else to be like God wants us to be. So, since you are Christians, we thought that you should be the ones in our church to remind everyone else what God wants them to be like. I want you to wear these tags that I am giving you on your shirts and dresses so that whenever anyone sees you he will always know that you are trying harder to bring happiness and peace to people in God's world. I know that I will remember better what I am supposed to be like if I see you wearing your tag that says, **WE TRY HARDER**.

Now that you know what the sign means, go and be people of peace and love.

EVIDENCE OF THE TRUTH

I Corinthians 1:4-9, verse 6: . . . because in you the evidence for the truth of Christ has found confirmation.

Object: Fingerprints on a glass, muddy shoes, cuff link with initial and some watermelon seeds.

Today I have a mystery for you. I want you to help solve it with me if you will. I have collected some evidence and I want to see if we can put it all together.

The other night I came home and I went out into the kitchen and I found a plate and a glass on the kitchen table. I wondered who had been eating at my table and I wanted to know what he had been eating. My first piece of evidence that I want to show you is this glass with some fingerprints on it. Next, I looked around and on the floor I saw some seeds, funny kinds of seeds that looked like this [**show them the watermelon seeds**] and so I picked them up and wrapped them very carefully in a napkin. Slowly and very carefully I began to walk around the house looking for more evidence. Sure enough, by the door there were some pretty muddy shoes that looked like they belonged to one of the children in my house. The person had been very careful to take them off so that he would not leave any tracks, but I remembered that it had rained not too long ago and where there was no grass it would still be muddy. I thought I knew who the shoes belonged to, but I still didn't know what he had eaten. Then I remembered our garden where I was keeping my prize watermelon. I ran to the place and looked. Oh, my heavens, it was gone! Now I knew what he had eaten and all I had to do was to match up the muddy shoes with the fingerprints and the very full tummy, plus the cufflinks I found near the scene with an initial on them, belonging to someone in my family, and I would have all the evidence that I needed to solve the mystery.

Well, you can probably guess who it was. There my boy lay, with a full tummy, a smile on his face, and some streaks of mud on his pants. Mystery solved and case closed! Now you see the evidence that I had collected was really important for it led me to the truth. Evidence is important and we need to look for the evidence before we make too many judgments.

That's what St. Paul said about Christians. He said that men and women who claim to be Christians leave a lot of evidence by which we can tell if they really follow Jesus or if they just say that they do. What is some of the evidence of being a Christian? People who are Christians care for all the people in the whole world, they love one another, they pray every day, they read their Bibles, they sing hymns of worship and enjoy being like Jesus. When you see that kind of person, you have the evidence -- enough evidence to know that he has the truth and is a Christian.

WORKING TOGETHER

Ephesians 4:17-28, verse 25: Therefore, putting away falsehood, let everyone speak the truth with his neighbor for we are members one of another.

Object: A flashlight or a transistor radio with one dead battery and several good ones. [Good one must be kept in reserve to replace the bad battery at the end of the story.]

Good morning, boys and girls. How are you on this very first Sunday in October? October is one of my favorite months of the year, for it is a month that shows lots of changes in God's world and we can see how active God is in nature. The leaves change color, some fall to the ground, the weather is very cool at night and bright and sunny during the day. It is a very good month.

I brought some friends with me today to help me tell you a story that I read in the Bible. First of all I want to show you Randy Radio. What a good friend Randy is to me. When I am all alone he speaks to me, plays good music, although sometimes he gets kind of loud, and once in a while I even listen to a ball game. Good old Randy. But every once in a while Randy stops playing and I don't know what to do. Oh, now I see. If I take the back off and look inside I will see a lot of Randy, and some of it will be bad. Does anyone know what might make Randy stop playing? [**Let them tell you about the batteries.**] Are all of the batteries bad? Maybe just one of them is bad. Well, lucky old Randy. I just happen to have another battery in my pocket, so we will take this one out and try the new battery in Randy. [**Make the bad battery the last one you try.**] Oh, there it is. Now Randy will work fine since all of the parts are good.

On the outside all of the batteries look the same, but one of them is bad. It keeps the whole radio from working right. So it is with people. St. Paul says that when one person lies it makes all of the people look bad. You may not think that it will hurt if you tell one little lie; but when you do, the Bible says that everyone, including you, is hurt because we all belong to each other. When one person in our church does wrong we all suffer.

So remember that you are just like one battery in Randy Radio. Be good and tell no lies and you will do your share to make our church work well together just as God wants it to.

THE RIGHT WAY

Ephesians 5:15-21, verse 15: Look carefully then how you walk, not as unwise men but as wise, making the most of the time, because the days are evil.

Object: An egg and a ball.

Good morning, boys and girls. Today we have a very special lesson to learn. It is one that we should know, but have a hard time learning. The lesson is about using our good sense and being careful. God tells us that we should use our brains and live sensibly and we won't get into trouble. There is a right way to do things and a wrong way. God says He has given us intelligence so that we can do them the right way. Let me show you what I mean.

Here is an egg. Over here we have a beautiful red ball.Now one of these you are supposed to bounce and the other one you are supposed to cook and eat. I am sure that if I use my good sense I will use each one for the right thing. But some people, even after they know what is right and what is wrong, still do the wrong thing. For instance,if I eat the ball and bounce the egg something is going to happen that I probably won't like.

Sometimes our parents tell us to pay attention in school so that we will learn. Or they say not to play with matches so that we won't get burned, or not to play with someone who is too big. Sometimes, even though we know they are right, we don't listen. When we don't listen we think we are special people and nothing can happen to us. That's the way I am when I have a pretty red ball and an egg. Would anyone like to eat my red ball while I bounce my egg? It is a delicious red ball. You see I am special and because I am special this egg won't break and that ball will taste good. Anyone here want to eat my red ball? Well, I am going to show you how my egg bounces. [**Drop egg in pan.**] Oh, my goodness, it didn't bounce. Not even for me. I must not be that special.

That's the way it is in this world. There are certain ways to live and to act. They are the same for all of us. God wants us to live the way He teaches us. He gives us good sense, and there is no other way.

So the next time you think that you want to do something that you know God disapproves of -- like lying, cheating, or being unkind to others -- remember that a ball doesn't taste good and an egg won't bounce, even for you. Use the good sense God gives you and **be careful!**

FINISHING WHAT WE START

2 Timothy 4:5-11, verse 7: I have fought the good fight, I have finished the race, I have kept the faith.

Object: Some knitting, a partially finished jigsaw puzzle, a scoreboard with only four innings completed out of nine.

Isn't this a wonderful day to be together? It's the middle of the month and all the leaves have now started to turn color. The air smells so good and on most days the sun is bright in the very blue sky. It surely is great the way God does things. Whatever He starts He finishes. That's the way He is.

Do you always finish everything you start? Do you ever just get something started when you think of something else to do and leave what you started on the floor or outside? [**Hold up the knitting.**] Here is my sweater. That's right, my wife started to knit me a sweater a couple of years ago and here it is today. How do you like that sweater? Do you think that sweater will keep me pretty warm? Now here is one of my favorite puzzles that I have been wanting to work on but my friend keeps telling me that I can have it back when he finishes it. I think he started this puzzle last Christmas. Oh, and there is one other thing that I brought along that really bothers me. The other night I went to a ball game and after the fourth inning it began to rain and, guess what? That's right, they still haven't finished it.

Finishing things is important. St. Paul says that he finished the race of life still a Christian. He doesn't talk about being the first one to finish or the strongest to finish. He is just able to say that he finished the race of life and he was still believing in the Lord Jesus Christ. I hope that all of you finish your life like St. Paul. Maybe some of you will be 100 or 125 or 90 or 65 when you finish. But it won't matter how old you are, as long as you finished a Christian.

It's a good lesson: finish what you start. You have all started as Christians and I hope you finish the same way. Don't be like my sweater, puzzle or ball game. Be like St. Paul -- finish what you start, particularly your Christian lives.

GOD BUYS US BACK

Romans 3:21-28, verse 24: . . . they are justified by his grace as a gift, through the redemption which is in Christ Jesus.

Object: A redemption center catalogue, some Top Value or Green Stamps and the gift.

Good morning, boys and girls. How are you today on this last Sunday of the month of October? It surely did go fast, didn't it?

Have you ever wondered about why Jesus died for us? If you have wondered, let me explain it in my own way. A long time ago God was thinking about how He could make all of the people part of His family again, just as they used to be before they started sinning. He had tried to make rules -- good rules, too -- but that didn't help because the people broke the rules. He looked and He looked and He looked at His people.

It reminds me how I feel when I look at one of these beautiful catalogues. I look and I look and I look and I just wish that I could buy one of these gifts. But all of the money in the world won't buy the gift. These stores just don't take money. But then one day a store gave me some stamps. The stamps looked like this. I went to the store and gave them my stamps and they gave me the gift I wanted.

Well, God was looking at His people and He finally decided on a plan. He decided that He would send His own Son, Jesus, into the world. Jesus would give his life, just as we give the stamps, only he would get people instead of gifts. Jesus is like a Top Value stamp. Only Jesus can make us ready for God. He redeems us. That's what Jesus does for us. He redeems us. When we are redeemed we belong to God again just as we did before we sinned. We can't buy redemption. Jesus can only give it to us and it is free. So remember what it means to be redeemed. It is God buying us back, not with money, or stamps or jewels but with the life of Jesus!

ALL SAINTS DAY

Revelation 7:2-17, verses 9 and 10: After this I looked, and behold, a great multitude which no man could number, from every nation, from all tribes and peoples and tongues, standing before the throne and before the Lamb, clothed in white robes, with palm branches in their hands, and crying out with a loud voice, "Salvation belongs to our God who sits upon the throne, and to the Lamb!"

Object: Different size rubberbands, toothpicks, newspaper, and a pack of mail.

Happy Halloween! I sure hope that not too many of you are sick this morning from eating all that spinach, green beans and liver. What's the matter? Didn't all of the people give you those good things when you went from house to house begging for treats? They didn't? What did they give you? [**Let them supply some answers.**] Well, I certainly gave away the wrong kind of things at my house. Yesterday was a special day for you, wasn't it?

Today is a special day in the Christian Church. It is called All Saints Day. How many of you know what a saint is, or what we mean when we use the word **saint**? [**Let them answer.**] Do any of you know someone who is called Saint? St. Peter and St. Paul, that's right. Are you a saint? Do you think that your mother and father are saints? Are all of the people in the church today saints? Well, they are if they believe that Jesus is the Son of God. That's right, a saint is a believer in Christ. You never thought that you were like St. Peter and Paul, did you?

Let me show you what I mean. I have here with me this morning something that all of you have seen before. [**Hold up rubberband.**] Randy Rubberband is so small that you

89

hardly even notice him. He is like a lot of Christians. You don't notice them for what they say or do but they are there and they believe and they have very important jobs. Look what Randy can do better than any other rubber band. [**Wrap it around some toothpicks.**] Randy can do that better than Roger Rubberband who I am holding now. But Robert is the kind of rubberband that my paper boy uses to wrap around the newspaper and helps him keep it together when he throws it on my porch.

Roger is like a few Christians we have heard of, like Martin Luther, Billy Graham, Calvin and some others.Very important people, but still rubberbands. There is one more friend I want to show you called Robert Rubberband and is he big! He will go all the way around this mail and you cannot miss him. He is like your St. Peter and St. Paul. There are not too many rubberbands like Robert, but he is still a rubberband.

That is the way it is with saints. Some of them do big jobs and everyone knows them. Some do little jobs and very few know them. But they are all believers in Jesus and that is why they are all saints.

THE PASSWORD IS "JESUS"

I Thessalonians 4:13-18, verse 14: For since we believe that Jesus died and rose again, even so, through Jesus, God will bring with Him those who have fallen asleep.

Object: The word "peace" or "love" or "hope" written on a card and kept, if possible, in a plastic cover to make it look like a password.

Good morning to you, boys and girls. The weather is changing so that we can tell the seasons are ending and beginning. Which season is half-way over and what season will soon be with us? That's right, the fall season is coming to a close and in another month the winter season will be with us. It is funny how things come and go. I suppose that is what makes the year and the weather so exciting.

Speaking of coming and going, I brought something with me this morning that I know all of you are going to like. Have you ever had a club that you and your friends belonged to, especially a secret club? If you have ever belonged to a secret club, you know there is something very important that everybody must know in order to get into the clubhouse to attend the meeting. What must every member know to get into the meeting? [**See if you can get the idea of the password from them.**] That's right, you must know the password. Sometimes we must memorize the password and other times we carry it with us in a little folder like this. [**Show them your folder.**]

The password today is hope. That's right, the password is hope and this morning when you leave church I am going to ask you the password and you will have to whisper it in my ear if you want to get out of church. O.K.? The password is hope.

Now, why do you think I shared this story with you this morning? You would never guess. Would you believe that **Jesus** is the password for all Christians after they die? That's right, Jesus is the password. The Bible tells us that God made Jesus our password into heaven. A lot of people wonder about what happens to them when they die and they no longer live on this earth. St. Paul says that there is nothing to worry about at all. God knew that there would have to be a special way and so He said that everyone should trust Jesus and he would make sure that everything went just right.

I hope that none of you ever worries about what is going to happen to you after you die. All of you believe in Jesus, and that is your password for eternal life.

HOW GOD WORKS FOR YOU

2 Peter 3:8-14, verse 9: The Lord is not slow about His promise as some count slowness, but is forebearing toward you, not wishing that any should perish, but that all should reach repentance.

Object: A small turtle [which can be purchased at any pet store] or a picture of a turtle.

Good morning, boys and girls. I hope that you are ready for a real surprise today. I have brought something with me that you could never guess in a thousand days or a thousand years. Would anyone like to guess what I have brought with me today? I will give you a hint. It is one of my special friends and his name is Timmy. Do you want to guess? [**Allow a few guesses.**] Give up? Well, let me show you who I have brought with me. Here, my friends, is Timothy Turtle. We call him Timmy for short and when he gets a little older we will call him Tim.

What do you know about Timmy Turtle and other friends like Tim? [**Let them tell you some things like the kind of food they eat, where they live and how they can snap.**] That is very good. Let me ask you one more thing. When you think of a turtle going someplace or doing something, what do you think about the speed he travels? Slow! If I told you that you ran like a turtle or did your work like a turtle, you would probably get pretty upset with me. A turtle is pretty slow about everything that it does. But did you know that a lot of turtles live to be quite old, some even older than people? I wonder if that is because when they move so slowly they don't make many mistakes.

Did you know that some people think that God moves like a turtle sometimes? They think that God moves more slowly than anybody they know. And you know what? I agree. Sometimes God moves very slowly because He wants to move slowly. It gives people a chance to think a little about the things they say and do and believe about God and other people. The Bible says that God gives men a chance to repent. Suppose God just reached down and socked you one on the chin every time you said something wrong or did something wrong? You sure would get a lot of socks, wouldn't you?

God isn't like that, is He? He gives you time to think about what you have done and change it if you have to or want to. God is very smart, much smarter than we are, and He knows what He is doing every second of the time. Sometimes it may seem like He is very slow, but then God never makes a mistake. He makes fewer than Timmy. So don't worry about how fast God works, just be glad that He is always working for you.

WAITING FOR JESUS

Romans 13:11-14, verse 11b: For salvation is nearer to us now than when we first believed.

Object: A driver's license.

Good morning, boys and girls. A very happy day to you. This is the first Sunday in Advent, which means that we are now preparing for the coming of Jesus Christ into the world again. That's right, we are here this morning to pray and hope that Jesus will come again, and that when he does we will know that the perfect world that God has planned has happened. The Bible says that the coming of Jesus into our world is closer to happening now than when we first heard about Jesus. Let me show you what I mean.

I want you to remember a couple of years ago when you were only two or three years old. How many of you can remember back to that time? Now I want you to think about your last birthday. Can you remember how old you were before your birthday? Good. Now how old must you be before you get one of these? [**Hold up driver's license.**] Do you know what I have here? A driver's license. How many of you would like to drive a car? All of you? You must be sixteen years old before you get to drive. Doesn't that seem like a long time to wait before you get to drive? Suppose that you are nine. You will have to wait seven years. Let's say that you are six years old. That means that you will have to wait ten years. Seven years, ten years, eight years -- they all seem like a long way away. But just think, you are closer to driving a car now than you were last year when you were only eight or five or seven.

That is the way it is with waiting for Jesus. Sometimes it seems like we talk about Jesus coming every year or even every Sunday and still he hasn't come. But just think how often you dream about being sixteen so that you can drive that car. While it seems like a long time away, I can promise you that it will happen. I can also promise you that one of these days Jesus will come, just like your driver's license, only you will be even happier with the coming of Christ.

So the thing that we **don't** have to do is worry. Just get ready for Jesus. You can't get any older by wishing it, but you can be ready when you become old enough. God asks all of us to wait and to be ready for Jesus.

LIVING TOGETHER IN HARMONY

Romans 15:4-13, verses 5 and 6: May the God of steadfastness and encouragement grant you to live in such harmony with one another, in accord with Christ Jesus, that together you may with one voice glorify the God and Father of our Lord Jesus Christ.

Object: A stamp pad and rubber stamp; a pen and pencil set; things that go together in harmony.

Well, boys and girls, we are in the last month of the year. It seems like the year only started a few days ago. The ends get so close to the beginnings that it seems like they are one. Of course, there are some pretty big things yet to happen this month, which I am sure you are aware of, so the month won't pass too quickly. Is there anything special happening in December that you are really looking forward to, like a special vacation or a birthday or anything like that? Christmas! What's that? [**Allow them to answer and get as many different answers as you can from them.**] It seems that everyone likes it, this thing called Christmas.

You remember that I said it seems like the end of the year and the beginning of the year come together? Most of the time we like things that go together. When time goes too fast, we don't like it because it seems like it is over before it begins. We don't like it either when the time seems to drag or go slow. But think of all the things that go better when they go together. How many of you like hamburgers? Great, but how many of you like hamburgers and ketchup? You like that even better!

I have brought some other things that go together. Look at what I have here. Some of these go together with one

97

thing but not with the others. For instance, you must know right away when you see this ink pad that it doesn't go with the pencil nor does the pen go with the ink pad. What belongs to the ink pad? That's right. The rubber stamp goes with the ink pad and the pen and pencil go together. We could say that they were in harmony with one another. When things that go together work well together in harmony, then everyone is happy.

Did you know that Jesus wants us to work together in harmony? He wants us to be happy with one another so that when we are happy we are praising God. That is what God teaches us, says St. Paul. We should live happily together. We should belong together like pencils and pens, and rubber stamps and ink pads belong together. God knows that if we are not happy with each other, then we will not be happy with ourselves. And if we are not happy with ourselves we will not love Him and worship Him.

It really is important, then, that we work together, doing things for one another, helping and caring not only for our own problems but also the problems of other people. When we are loving each other then our hearts will be like one loud voice praising God in harmony.

IN THE DARK

I Corinthians 4:1-5, verse 5: Therefore do not pronounce judgment before the time, before the Lord comes, who will bring to light the things now hidden in darkness and will disclose the purposes of the heart. Then every man will receive his commendation from God.

Object: Cup your hands with thumbs together leaving only a small dark hole to look into. Take any small object that will remain unseen in the dark. Try to get the children to make a judgment on what they see while it is still in darkness.

This morning, boys and girls, I am going to need some volunteers for a little experiment. I am going to need some people who have very good eyesight -- excellent eyesight. Is there anyone here who can see very well, so well that even in dark rooms you can make out some things? Well, now, let's see. I will choose this one who believes that he can see very well and I will also choose this boy who wears glasses that allow him to see extra well.

I am going to cup my hands like this and leave a very little hole into which you can look and see. Now the idea is to look into the hole and tell me what you think you see. [**Let each one take a look before you ask.**] I realize that it is pretty dark, but you both told me that you could see well in the dark, so will you please tell me what you have seen? Let's ask our girl to go first. [**See if you can get them to commit themselves to a specific thing. If they only say that they can't see, then you will have to get some other volunteers.**] Are you sure that is what you see, or would you like to take another look? That's good peeking you are doing. Do you want to stick with your first answer or do

99

you want to change your mind?

Now let's see what I have in my hand. A paper clip! No one said a paper clip or anything that even looks like a paper clip. You know what? I knew that no one was going to tell me what I had in my hand because inside that little hole that I made with my fingers there is only darkness. It is only with light that we are able to see.

Now I want to tell you why I did this little experiment. People make the same kind of mistakes about other people and themselves that our two friends made here this mornig. People make judgments about each other without ever knowing what the reasons were for doing or saying something. God says to us that we should not judge each other, that we must wait for Jesus to make that judgment. Only Jesus has enough light to see why something was said or done. When Jesus comes it will be like opening my hand to the light. When my hand is shut with only a little hole it is like our trying to make a judgment. We think we see and think we understand, but we don't have enough information.

The next time you get ready to judge a friend or think of him badly, remember what it is like to look through a little hole into darkness, and how different it is to see with light. Then you will know that it is only for God to judge and that will happen when Jesus returns to earth.

A SURE CURE FOR WORRY

Philippians 4:4-7, verse 6: Have no anxiety about anything, but in everything by prayer and supplication with thanksgiving let your requests be made known to God.

Object: Pills, pills, and more pills.

It is only five more days till Christmas and I am worried. I am so worried I don't know what to do. I am worried about not having my Christmas shopping done and I am sure that I have forgotten someone. I had better take a pill for those worries. [**Take some candy pills or simply a bottle of pills out of a bag and set them down for each worry.**] Then I have to remember to get all of the things ready for our Christmas dinner and I worry about forgetting the turkey or mince pie. I had better take a pill for that worry. Then I worry about getting to church on time on Christmas Eve. Is there a pill for that? Oh, of course, right here is a pill for those who worry about being late. Well, I like a white Christmas, and so I worry about the snow coming on the 24th of December. Is there a snow pill? Sure, there is the snow pill. I worry about the needles on the Christmas tree falling off before Christmas day and so I must take a pill for that. There are other things that I have pills for, like one to get me to sleep on Christmas Eve and one to take after I eat too much for Christmas dinner, and one to take when the noise gets too loud and so forth. Pill, pills, pills. Worry, worry, worry.

How many of you worry like that? It seems kind of silly, doesn't it? But that is the way it is with many people. They may not take that many pills, but they worry that much. You know what? St. Paul knew people who used to worry about a lot of things. He said that he had a great cure for worriers. It wasn't pills, or biting your fingernails, or walking up and down over the same area. Instead he told them to pray. That's right, pray.

St. Paul said that if you had anything that was bothering you and it started to make your worry, you should go to God. You should tell Him what it was that you were bothered about and thank Him for taking care of it and for listening to you. How about that? That must mean if God is going to take care of my worrying, I will have more time to do the things that I want to do. Isn't it amazing the way God works? I know why St. Paul was always praising God and singing hymns about Him. Paul had so much time to do the things that he wanted to do because God took all of his worry and problems and answered his prayers with joy and love.

The next time I have something that bothers me, I am going to quit worrying and start praying. Then I will have time to get the gifts, the turkey, and the right tree. I will be at church on time and I will be glad whether it snows or there is sunshine. This is going to be a beautiful week without any worry.

LET'S GIVE A CHEER!

I John 1:1-10, verse 3: That which we have seen and heard we proclaim also to you so that you may have fellowship with us, and our fellowship is with the Father and with His Son Jesus Christ.

Object: An athletic cheer ["Jones, Jones, he's our man; if he can't do it, nobody can!"]

Well, boys and girls, we have come to the very last Sunday in the year. Hasn't it been great to spend 52 times togeathe ? Think of all the things we have heard and learned about Jesus. Do you remember some of the favorite stories that you heard about Jesus? Who would like to tell me his favorite story about something that Jesus did or said? [**Select a volunteer. Help with the story if necessary and get some common agreement on the fact that it was a good story.**] Very good! We really do enjoy being together, don't we? I think one of the best parts of worshipping God is that it allows us to come together and talk about our Lord Jesus.

How many of you have ever been to a football game? Some of you have and some of you have not. Would you pretend with me this morning that we were all going to a game? When we go to a game we are all going to sit together. Right? And while we are there we will eat some hot dogs, drink some hot chocolate and try to stay together. We probably won't know many of the people who are at the game, so we have to stay together. Do you like to go many places where you don't know the people? I don't either. You don't feel like you belong. The last time I went to a game and I didn't know anybody, I just sat there and watched and it really wasn't much fun. The other people jumped up and down and cheered and I just sat there. Say,

Say, I know what we can do. We can have a cheer just like the other people. As a matter of fact, I know some of the cheers that the people at the game will be cheering and we could learn it right now before we go. Then I think we will feel like we belong. Let's see if you can follow me. [**Say it line by line a couple of times, building with enthusiasm each time.**] O.K., now let's try it . . . Very good.

It makes you feel like you belong. I feel better about going to our pretend game now than I did before. Don't you?

That's the way it is with being a Christian. One of the reasons we like to share all the stories that we know about Jesus is that it makes us all feel like we belong. It is the same way with hymns and prayers and coming to church and standing around before and afterward and talking to each other. It makes us feel like we belong. That is why Jesus wants us to tell everyone everything that we know about God because He is everybody's Father. We should all know what you know.

Do you understand why it is imortant that we tell everyone what we have seen and heard about Jesus so they will know him as we know him? It's just like knowing the cheers at a football game. When they cheer, we will cheer, too. We will share the fun of cheering together, and we will all feel that we belong.

Happy New Year!